#THOUGHT LEADERSHIP **tweet** Book01

140 Prompts for Designing and Executing an Effective Thought Leadership Campaign

Liz Alexander, PhD and Craig Badings

Foreword by Jeff Ernst, Principal Analyst, Forrester Research

E-mail: info@thinkaha.com
20660 Stevens Creek Blvd., Suite 210
Cupertino, CA 95014

Published by THiNKaha®, a Happy About® imprint
20660 Stevens Creek Blvd., Suite 210, Cupertino, CA 95014
http://thinkaha.com

Second Printing: October 11, 2012
First Printing: October 4, 2012
Paperback ISBN: 978-1-61699-092-3 (1-61699-092-9)
eBook ISBN: 978-1-61699-093-0 (1-61699-093-7)
Place of Publication: Silicon Valley, California, USA
Paperback Library of Congress Number: 2012935565

Trademarks

Warning and Disclaimer

Advance Praise

"This book echoes my view that people don't care about products! Thought leadership engages buyers about what matters to them, not your ego."
David Meerman Scott, Bestselling Author, *The New Rules of Marketing and PR*

"An excellent guide; using Twitter to show how thought leadership should be done, written by two leading experts in the field."
Dr. Fiona Czerniawska, Co-founder, Source for Consulting

"If Confucius was a marketer, he would be tweeting proverbs like Alexander & Badings do on thought leadership."
Dale Bryce, Group Manager, Marketing, Sinclair Knight Merz

"This book is thought haiku. It asks penetrating questions about the how, why, and what of leveraging the biggest B2B marketing idea around."
Matt Church, Founder, Thought Leaders Global

"Everyone wants to be a thought leader today, but can they? *#THOUGHT LEADERSHIP tweet* delivers a concise overview of what it really takes."
Eric Wittlake, Senior Director of Media, Babcock & Jenkins, Inc.

"Chock-full of tidbits that spark ideas for pursuing thought leadership! If thought leadership is one of your spear points, carry this book with you at all times."
Mignon van Halderen, Assistant Professor, Corporate Communication, Rotterdam School of Management, Erasmus University, Holland

Dedication

Thought leadership may not have been a concept with which they were familiar, but no one taught me more about the value of innovative thinking and who exemplified leadership than my parents.

To Jimmy and Joyce Alexander—I can never thank you enough for preparing me so well for this wonderful, creatively fulfilling life.

Liz Alexander, PhD

Dedication (continued...)

I'd like to dedicate this book to those business people brave enough to give thought leadership a go. I have witnessed first-hand the power of thought leadership done properly. I have been a convert ever since and have immersed myself in everything to do with the discipline. I hope that this book acts as a catalyst, guide, and inspiration to all aspiring thought leaders out there.

Craig Badings

Acknowledgments

We are grateful to all those people whose thought leadership expertise has helped inform our thinking about this fascinating topic, as well as who so graciously and generously took the time to review, offer helpful insights, and/or praise the content of this book. They include: Marte Semb Aasmundsen, Dale Bryce, Bob Buday, Matt Church, Dr. Fiona Czerniawska, Jeff Ernst, Dave Gardner, Mignon van Halderen, Dana VanDen Heuvel, Erica Levy Klein, Britton Manasco, David Meerman Scott, and Eric Wittlake.

Thanks also to Mitchell Levy, Rajesh Setty, Diane Vo, and the rest of the Happy About® team for the opportunity to expound upon a topic we are both so passionate about and for the support they have given to the development and promotion of *#THOUGHT LEADERSHIP tweet*.

--

Craig, I'd like to thank you for showing me that two heads *are* better than one, and for such a joyful co-authorship experience. I sincerely appreciate your generosity of spirit and the chance to learn even more about thought leadership from you.

Liz Alexander, PhD

Liz, thanks for your constant enthusiasm and for inviting me to be part of this exciting process. The collaboration has made this book truly better for it. The many weekend and early morning Skype calls were stimulating and productive. Here's to the next one!

Craig Badings

How to Read This THiNKaha® Book
A Note from the Publisher

The THiNKaha series was devised as a modern day CliffsNotes on a broad range of business topics and related skills. Each THiNKaha book advocates life-long learning in order to help you transform the "aha" moments they inspire into actionable items with tangible results.

Within *#THOUGHT LEADERSHIP tweet* the authors have maintained the overall vision and goals of the series, but with some key differences. Here's how to get the most out of this particular book.

1. Read through this THiNKaha book (this slim and handy volume should only take 30-40 minutes of your time), especially noting those aspects of thought leadership that were surprising, contradicted your current understanding, or required special attention for you or your organization.

2. Each of the seven discrete sections builds on the others to help you think through all the essential elements of an effective organizational thought leadership campaign. Each section contains a series of prompts (140 in total) to provoke discussions about thought leadership with your senior management, team, and external partners.

3. Where relevant, check out the QR Codes assigned to some of the prompts. Use this supplemental information (case studies, additional resources, etc.) to gain further understanding about that particular issue.

4. Address and develop action items around the issues raised by these prompts, drawing on the examples and suggestions at the end of each section for further inspiration.

5. Review the five-stage "Thought Leadership Blueprint" offered in the Appendix and use that guidance to help inform your actions.

6. Encourage your team (and be sure to do this yourself) to identify what "aha!" moments these prompts helped to inspire. Please share these with the authors (see "About the Authors" for their contact information) to help us ensure that future books in the THiNKaha *#THOUGHT LEADERSHIP tweet* series communicate best practice.

7. Refer to this book regularly, to help maintain the quality of thought leadership that you, your clients, and your industry deserve.

As CEO of THiNKaha, I definitely practice what I preach. I read *#CORPORATE CULTURE tweet*, *#LEADERSHIP tweet*, *#TEAMWORK tweet* and this new addition—*#THOUGHT LEADERSHIP tweet*—once a month and take away two to three different action items from each of them every time. Please email me your "aha!" moments, too.

Mitchell Levy, CEO
publisher@thinkaha.com

Contents

Foreword by Jeff Ernst, Principal Analyst, Forrester Research

"Thought leadership marketing doesn't just educate potential buyers about an issue; it provides a strong point of view that brings new insight and thinking to an issue. Any B2B company that solves complex problems should create a set of strategic objectives, resources, and processes that make thought leadership happen.

"Companies that lack a process or framework find themselves practicing random acts of thought leadership. They react to industry and customer issues in an ad hoc manner rather than proactively planning a cohesive thought leadership platform."

From "Thought Leadership: The Next Wave Of Differentiation In B2B Marketing" (June 7, 2011) by Jeff Ernst, Principal Analyst, Forrester Research

Introduction
What Is Thought Leadership?

In the late 1990s, editor Joel Kurtzman came up with a collective noun for the cutting edge thinkers who were contributing insights to a series of interviews appearing in Booz & Company's *strategy+business*. Kurtzman called these people "thought leaders."

Among "the world's most innovative and distinguished executives, authors, and academicians" included in Kurtzman's book, *Thought Leaders: Insights on the Future of Business*, were Warren Bennis, John T. Chambers, Charles Handy, Minoru Makihara, and C.K. Prahalad.[1]

Since then the concept of "thought leadership" has broadened. Many consultants began adopting the term, believing it was synonymous with calling themselves *trusted advisors, subject matter experts*, or even *futurists*. But "thought leader" is not a position *you* choose to adopt, it is bestowed on you by others.

Thought leaders advance the marketplace of ideas by positing actionable, commercially relevant, research-backed, *new* points of view. They engage in "blue ocean strategy" thinking on behalf of themselves and their clients, as opposed to simply churning out product-focused, brand-centric white papers or curated content that shares or mimics others' ideas.

While individual thought leaders are in plentiful supply, organizations continue to struggle to establish their thought leadership; it is for this reason that we decided to write this book. It will help you consider all the elements necessary to design and execute a successful thought leadership campaign.

---

1. Joel Kurtzman, *Thought Leaders: Insights on the Future of Business* (San Francisco, CA: Jossey-Bass, 1998).

In today's uncertain, ever-changing environment, we need to listen more, understand better, and re-energize our relationships with increasingly discerning, demanding, and skeptical customers and clients. This means that *you* need to differentiate your organization with compelling points of view that are intriguing, innovative, inspiring, and wholly relevant to your audience.

Truly powerful thought leadership campaigns are embedded into the culture of the organization; they're not simply communication "add-ons." The most effective thought leadership initiatives empower all employees by inspiring and supporting them to become campaign ambassadors. They also contribute a depth of insight into internal and external conversations that your competitors can only dream of achieving. We're not talking about PR, advertising, or product marketing here, but a *change management approach*—as you will discover as you work your way through this book.

Many organizations are squandering time, money, and effort on thought leadership initiatives that do not move the needle in terms of establishing a differentiated brand identity, deep trust, and loyal followership. Armed with this small yet immensely powerful book, that will no longer be your concern!

Following a brief introduction, each of the seven sections contains a number of tweet-sized prompts that will help you address many of the issues frequently overlooked by aspiring thought leaders. Use these questions to provoke discussions not only within your senior team but with those people you identify as potential thought leadership champions. Directly after the prompts, we provide you with examples to help you shift from reflective mode into action. Plus, at the close of this book—in the Appendix (page 143)—we present our proven, five-stage "Thought Leadership Blueprint" that outlines all the steps you need to take to leverage your thoughts and resources.

Section 1

What Does It Take to Become a Thought Leader?

Individuals and organizations call themselves "thought leaders" all the time. But what really counts is whether your clients, customers, and competitors recognize you as such. To give you the best chance of success with your thought leadership initiative, there are some preliminary questions you should be asking yourself. The following prompts will help you identify the cultural underpinning (prevailing attitudes as well as available resources) that make or break thought leadership campaigns.

1

What is your
organization's definition
of thought leadership?
How does that differ from
being trusted advisors or
subject matter experts?

2

Have you defined
clearly what thought
leadership means to your
organization and what you
want to achieve from it?

3

To what extent do you have senior management support for the proposed thought leadership campaign, and where's the evidence of that?

4

Do you agree that it
is better not to embark on a
thought leadership campaign
at all than to do it poorly?

5

Is everyone on board with implementing a long-term, culture-based strategy, not just a short-term marketing fix? How do you know that?

6

How brave are you prepared
to be in terms of putting forward
potentially controversial or
challenging points of view?

7

Have sufficient budget and resources
been allocated for this thought
leadership campaign? Does that
include plenty of time to think?

8

A hallmark of true thought leadership is the confidence to take the route that 99.9 percent of industry experts don't even see. Will you?

9

Does your organization have a culture of listening and what mechanisms have you put in place to truly listen to your market's needs?

10

Will your research brief deliver an end result that is easily translated into client-friendly thought leadership material?

11

Thought leadership means owning an issue while generously sharing your ideas. Does that approach sit well within your existing culture?

12

What internal concerns might there be about giving away so much intellectual capital? How will you allay those fears?

13

Thought leadership is the willingness to go one way when most people are going the other. Does your culture support that?

14

Is your environment supportive of a culture of innovation? How have you demonstrated that in the past?

15

An innovative culture accepts failure as part of the way great ideas are born. Does yours?

16

General Patton once said, "If everyone is thinking alike, someone isn't thinking." How differentiated is the thinking in your organization?

17

Do you admire the late, great Steve Jobs but no way in hell would hire anyone like him? Do innovators thrive or die in your culture?

18

Ever wonder how some iconoclasts think differently? Nobel prize-winning physicist Richard Feynman studied things with no answers.

19

Thought leadership means expanding the boundaries of existing thinking. What fresh perspectives might you be overlooking?

20

Is your thought leadership brand agnostic? Do you realize that if it is too brand or product-centric, your thought leadership loses value?

21

Which members of your team will challenge your organization's assumptions in order to engage in truly breakthrough thinking?

22

Who are your internal thought leadership champions? Why have you chosen these people? Have you drawn from a diverse range of thinkers?

23

How far do the values of your organization align with your thought leadership point of view?

24

Will your thought leadership topic have long-term potential? The campaigns that benefit clients and organizations best run for many years.

Putting Into Practice

In order to clarify whether you are ready to move forward with an effective thought leadership approach, here are three areas on which to focus your preliminary discussions:

1. Environment (having a supportive culture)
2. Strategy (how this campaign aligns with your overall vision and mission)
3. People (who is on board?)

Environment: Innovative thinking requires a supportive environment: a culture that encourages and facilitates cross-disciplinary meetings and sharing of information, as well as a willingness to encourage, accept, and learn from the ups and downs of your creative endeavors.

Cultures that exemplify thought leadership don't proscribe expectations, such as, "Have that thought leadership report on my desk by 5:00 p.m. today!" or "Produce some new ideas to help generate leads for the next quarter."

Weekly product-focused white papers, regularly curated content, PR responses to an industry-related development, or news reports may provide value to your clients. But the disciplined, time-consuming, iconoclastic thinking that defines true thought leadership is nurtured in a very different setting.

Strategy: Thought leadership needs to be recognized as a business-wide alignment between new ways of thinking and your organization's mission and vision. It should never be reduced to a mere communications or marketing tool.

For your thought leadership to be strategically effective, it has to be client-centric. If you are not addressing a client or industry-specific issue with new thinking, your thought leadership runs the risk of being merely one of the thousands of pieces of self-serving content out there.

Think long-term! Make sure your thought leadership campaign is set up for success by aligning it with the bigger picture goals of the entire organization, not just the short-term needs of sales and marketing.

People: Ensure there is sufficient differentiated thinking within your organization. You are ideally looking for people who know how to ask great questions—the kind of questions that will potentially shine a light on unchartered areas of growth and profitable exploration for your customers or clients.

If you have insufficient numbers of bold thinkers in your organization—people who are not afraid to challenge the status quo—and you are serious about thought leadership, consider revising your recruitment strategy to attract them. Alternatively, partner with organizations, business associations, or academic institutions that are already populated with people who can provoke you to think differently about your business or industry. Wherever you find those courageous enough to take your organization and clients into previously unexplored territory, trust them and back them with the right resources.

Section II

What Impact Do You Want This Campaign to Achieve?

As the late Dr. Stephen Covey outlined as habit #2 in his book, *The 7 Habits of Highly Effective People*, "Begin with the end in mind."[2] The tweet-sized prompts offered in this section are designed to help you address *why* you are considering implementing a thought leadership campaign, what's in it for you, and, more importantly, what's in it for your clients. In particular, they will help you explore, discuss, and articulate your thought leadership objectives as they align with your organization's overall goals.

2. Stephen R. Covey, *The 7 Habits of Highly Effective People* (New York: Simon and Schuster, 1989).

25

Have you clearly mapped out with senior management what you want to achieve from your thought leadership strategy?

26

Simon Sinek[3] said, "It doesn't matter what you do. It matters why you do it."[4] Why are you embarking on a thought leadership campaign?

---

3. *Start With Why*, http://www.startwithwhy.com.
4. Simon Sinek, *Start with Why: How Great Leaders Inspire Everyone to Take Action* (New York: Portfolio, 2009).

27

To what extent does your proposed campaign align with your business objectives? What needs to be modified in order to ensure that it does?

28

How is your thought leadership campaign going to generate new revenue for your business over the next 12 to 36 months?

29

Rosabeth Moss Kanter said, "Act bigger than you are. Claim territory with a big impact goal."[5] What will that mean for you?

5. Rosabeth Moss Kanter, "Act Bigger than You Are," *Harvard Business Review* (blog), July 17, 2012 (8:08 a.m.), http://bit.ly/Act_Bigger.

30

What brand perception do you want to leave with your clients or prospects without your campaign becoming too brand or product-centric?

31

Thought leaders imagine a desired outcome then ask what has to happen to achieve it. They play "what if?" backwards. Do you?

32

Have you clearly defined who you want to reach with this thought leadership campaign and why?

33

When prospects currently compare you with your competitors, are you clearly differentiated? How will your campaign contribute to that goal?

34

What is it you want your target audience to do when they receive or interact with your thought leadership point of view?

35

What do your current clients say about you? Why is that, and how do you want this campaign to enhance that perception?

36

What kind of world do your clients want? What unrealized possibilities could you seek out on their behalf?

37

To enhance your impact further, what third party endorser (such as a credible industry body or academic institution) might you partner with?

38

Have you thought about how your thought leadership campaign could be used to attract and retain the best talent in your industry?

39

In preparation for knowing how to measure the impact of this campaign, are you clear on what success looks like externally and internally?

40

Today's consumer is in fact a "contsumer"[6]—someone who is hungry for content to help make decisions. Does your content play to them?

6. Craig Badings, "Your content will die if you don't shift your paradigm," *Thought Leadership* (blog), December 6, 2011, http://tinyurl.com/8uvs56p.

41

Do you clearly understand your clients' issues and what keeps them awake at night? Will your thought leadership address some or all of them?

42

Erica Levy Klein[7] asks, "Are you integrating your thought leadership strategically into your business development and marketing efforts?"

7. *Erica Klein,* http://www.thoughtleadershipwriter.com.

43

If you want to make a real impact with clients, constantly ask if your thought leadership is about them. Does it address *their* needs?

44

Want to understand thought
leadership from a marketer's
point of view? Visit Dana
VanDen Heuvel's site.[8]

8. "Search results for 'thought leadership,'" *Marketing Savant*,
   http://bit.ly/thought_leadership.

45

Have you thought about the impact you want your thought leadership campaign to have on your employees? If not, what will you do about that?

46

Is your firm ready to generate new revenues from your thought leadership initiative? Take Erica Levy Klein's "TL Readiness" quiz[9] & find out.

9. Erica Levy Klein, "10 Point Quiz: Is Your Company Ready to Generate New Revenue From a Thought Leadership Program?" ThoughtLeadershipWriter.com, **http://www.thoughtleadershipwriter.com/Quiz.aspx#quiz**.

Putting Into Practice

Thought leadership initiatives often suffer the same fate that many social media campaigns do when they are embarked upon for their own sake. Too many organizations are setting up social media profiles "because everyone else is doing it," which is why many are not seeing the return on investment (ROI) for which they had hoped.

Someone in your organization may have suggested embarking on a thought leadership campaign because your competitors are in on the action. But you need to find your own reasons for embarking on this journey.

Consider, for example, the different outcomes experienced by these three organizations:

1. Sinclair Knight Merz (SKM) is an engineering firm that uses its thought leadership to develop real depth of understanding and deep insights about its clients' businesses and sectors. It is intended to deliver something of value to SKM's clients way beyond the services it sells in order to position itself as a partner of choice.

2. Booz & Company has conducted the Global Innovation 1000 study every year since 2005, in which it investigates the relationship between the amount companies spend on research and development and their overall financial performance. Booz & Company engages in this thought leadership to drive media coverage, raise the profile of its consulting abilities in the innovation space, and secure speaking engagements.

3. Deloitte Australia has focused on boardroom risk for over six years. Its view is that a thought leadership campaign is a door opener, enabling top level, strategic conversations with clients and prospects. Clients buy this expertise, but it is Deloitte's thought leadership position that helped establish that expertise in the first place.

Be sure to emphasize in your preliminary discussions what you want this thought leadership campaign to achieve for your organization. Identify at the outset how your thought leadership objectives fit with the bigger picture goals of your organization so that your campaign is strategically effective. Use the START IP approach we outline in the Appendix of this book (see page 143) to help with that.

Section III

How Will You Know You've Succeeded?

Don't make the mistake of waiting until the conclusion of your campaign to gauge whether it was successful or not. By determining what measures you need to put in place at the outset, you can continually make informed adjustments and tweaks along the way. This will help ensure the best possible returns from the time, effort, and financial resources invested in your thought leadership campaign. Use the following tweet-sized prompts to provoke discussions around how best to measure, evaluate, and recalibrate your campaign.

47

Will your thought leadership motivate your target audience to act or change the paradigms of your industry or market sector?

48

Is everyone clear that thought leadership is not just about generating new ideas but ones that are relevant & actionable for your audience?

49

How will you avoid suffering the all-too-common mistake of being data rich but insight poor with respect to your thought leadership metrics?

50

The expert thinks, "How can this strengthen my position?" The thought leader thinks, "How can this enhance my clients' position?"

51

In what ways are you flexible enough to modify this campaign throughout to bolster its chances of success?

52

Are you set up to
only measure the end result?
How will you measure
incremental changes so
you can celebrate wins
and recalibrate as you go?

53

What relevant measures do you have in place to capture the coverage, online mentions, and impact of your thought leadership campaign?

54

How do you plan to measure the internal (not just external) effects of your thought leadership campaign?

55

Who will be responsible for measuring the impact of your campaign and will they have access to all the data they need?

56

Have you created and communicated a detailed briefing document for all the parties involved, outlining expectations and deliverables?

57

What Key Performance Indicators[10] do you have across all aspects of your thought leadership campaign? Are they practical & measurable?

10. Bernard Marr, "What is a Key Performance Indicator (KPI)?"
   Advanced Performance Institute,
   http://bit.ly/Key_Performance_Indicator.

58

Will everyone associated with your thought leadership efforts know the Key Performance Indicators and their individual contributions?

59

You get what you reward. Is your reward structure set up to strategically align with the success metrics for this campaign?

60

How are you working with HR to embed individual Key Performance Indicators (KPIs) that dovetail with your campaign's overall KPIs?

61

Are you focusing on what is measurable to the exclusion of what is possible? Don't allow metrics to dictate what is explored.

62

Are you hampered by
the "ICE" approach to
measuring success? (See
"The problems with KPIs".[11])

---

11. Ibid.

63

Bob Buday[12] asks,

"Are you using thought

leadership as R&D for service

innovation, as this is the Holy

Grail of thought leaders?"

_____

12. *The Bloom Group*, http://www.bloomgroup.com.

64

What quantitative and qualitative measures of this thought leadership campaign are you capturing?

Putting Into Practice

By now you should be clear that effectively measuring the impact of your thought leadership campaign requires identifying key metrics from the outset. In planning your campaign, you will need to carefully define the objectives, gain senior management buy-in, and then determine how you will measure success.

Let's illustrate this with an example: Booz & Company's Innovation 1000 Global Campaign.

Its objectives are threefold:

1. Showcase Booz & Company within the top tier business media worldwide as a leader in innovation thinking and research.
2. Provide an effective vehicle to interest and engage clients and prospective clients.
3. Secure speaking engagements.

Booz & Company measures these outcomes by:

- Tracking media coverage, social media mentions, and traffic to booz.com and strategy-business.com.
- Tracking the interest, leads, and sales generated directly and indirectly as a result of Innovation 1000.
- Comparing the speaking engagements it secured against the number it had in previous years.

These measurement criteria don't apply to every thought leadership campaign, of course. Here are some other outcomes you might measure:

- Visits to website content: video views, e-book/white paper downloads, etc.
- E-mail click-through rates.
- Attendance at talks, webinars, and conferences.
- Twitter, LinkedIn, Facebook followers, connections, and fans.
- Third party endorsement of your thought leadership point of view.
- Media coverage across tier one (mainstream) and tier two (trade) media; measuring tone and accuracy of key messages.
- New prospect engagement.
- Researched client feedback.
- Internal impact (e.g., How do employees view it? How do they use it? Is it used to prompt conversations with clients?).
- Changes to brand reputation indices.
- Google rankings on agreed search terms.

One final word of advice on this issue: avoid measuring only what is easy to measure, such as how many additional media mentions your thought leadership content attracts. This tends to be the default for most organizations. What you want to determine is the *impact* your thought leadership efforts are having in steering clients and customers toward territory that will have major benefits for them and for you.

Section IV

What Space Has Already Been Claimed?

We cannot stress enough the importance of research in your thought leadership journey. Once you've identified the key issues affecting your customers' or clients' lives, it's critical that you discover what conversations are already taking place. After all, avenues that you think represent potential thought leadership topics may already be "owned" by someone else. Consider the following questions to help you determine who is saying what in your industry or market sector, including using content creation as a vital preliminary step to discovering your unique thought leadership point of view.

65

When did you last research your market's issues and challenges? Who is currently answering these through their thought leadership, and how?

66

Have you overlooked how content curation helps you better understand, attract, and engage the audience you want for your thought leadership?

67

What key trends are impacting your clients? Can these inform your thought leadership or is someone else already providing insights on these?

68

Imagine yourself in the shoes of a key client or customer. What are the pressing issues on your mind and how are others solving them?

69

Have you considered how curating others' content helps boost brand visibility as a precursor to launching your thought leadership campaign?

70

For what do you want to be known? Does this deliver a thought leadership opportunity aligned with your values and your clients' issues?

71

Have you searched globally and locally for all possible content in the thought leadership space you have identified?

72

Are you curating others' content wisely to help complement the new, fresh perspectives of your emerging thought leadership?

73

What search terms and tracking tools are you using to map the potential point of view in which you are interested?

74

Within the broad thought leadership space someone else owns, is there a niche area you can claim?

75

Are you equipped to curate content? Remember its value in helping you stay in touch with trends to inform your thought leadership topics.

76

An overcrowded thought leadership space is an oxymoron. Are you prepared to let go of a good idea if someone else got there first?

77

Did you know that almost 85 percent of marketing executives cited thought leadership as their primary objective for content curation?[13]

---

13. "Content Curation Can Inform, Engage Customers," *eMarketer*," June 4, 2012, **http://bit.ly/Content_Curation_Article**.

78

Eric Wittlake asks,

"Are you confusing respect & attention with thought leadership in the hope of shortcutting through content curation?"[14]

_____

14. Eric Wittlake, "Three Reasons Content Curation Is Overrated," *B2B Digital Marketing* (blog), June 11, 2012, http://bit.ly/Content_Curation_Overrated.

79

How might this Vistage
article by Brent Gleeson[15]
help you connect the dots
between content curation
and thought leadership?

---

15. Brent Gleeson, "Thought Leadership 'Links' to SEO: Gain
Powerful Natural Links Through Respect & Reputation,"
Executive Street (Vistage.com blog), July 17, 2012,
http://bit.ly/Thought_Leadership_Links.

Putting Into Practice

To emphasize the value of the learning and insights that were hopefully provoked by the prompts offered in this section, let us consider a couple of examples to demonstrate how best to proceed.

If you were operating in the health and beauty sector, we would not advocate positioning yourself as a thought leader around the topic of "real beauty" because this is an area well leveraged by Dove® with their Campaign for Real Beauty. Likewise, the theme of innovation is to a large extent owned by the management consultancy, Booz & Company. If you were a management consultant, you would probably battle to gain traction in that space. But as a specialist plastics manufacturer, you could well explore and own a niche thought leadership space in the area of plastics innovation.

The importance of establishing your thought leadership in an area no one else owns (in order to showcase new and innovative thinking) can also be illustrated by considering what would happen if someone tried to emulate IBM's Smarter Planet campaign. By trying to position themselves in this already "taken" space, newcomers would run the risk of being labeled a follower at best or a plagiarist at worst.

These examples illustrate how important it is to engage in thorough research before thinking about establishing your thought leadership niche. Make it a point to conduct extensive global searches around relevant topics using Google or other search engines, and do a "deep dive" within the websites of your major competitors to identify what they are doing in that thought leadership space.

Bear in mind that whereas thought leadership is *not* synonymous with content curation, the development of a unique point of view often emerges from consistently reviewing what others are saying about issues of interest and importance to your clients or prospects. Take the time to analyze others' content, but make sure you add something new before sharing it with your audience. Preferably back up this different perspective with your own research or a partner's research.

Content curation serves two purposes: it brings top-of-mind awareness in terms of the value you are adding to the conversation; and it helps you discover, inform, and articulate your thought leadership point of view. Regularly curating content can also help you keep track of what your competitors and others are saying, provoking you to even greater heights of innovative thinking.

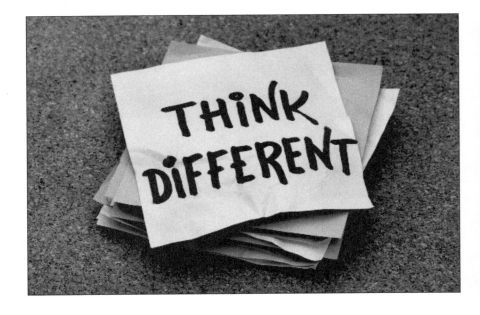

Section V

What Will Be Your Unique Point of View?

At its core, thought leadership is about two things:

1. Identifying one or more client-centric issues or challenges—especially ones your clients (and your competitors) don't see coming.

2. Devising an innovative approach that will anticipate, solve, or lessen the effects of these challenges.

Do these two things superbly and you will become indispensable and trusted, and sell more products and services. Are you ready to provoke yourself and your team to truly differentiate yourselves? The following prompts will help you do just that.

80

What keeps your clients or
prospects awake at night?
Why? How can you use
this to inform your thought
leadership point of view?

81

What can you share with your target audience that they don't already know and would not have thought of themselves?

82

Are you examining your own thinking and how you are processing your information internally to arrive at a thought leadership position?

83

Anticipate "black swans."[16] What rare, random, unplanned yet market-defining and game-changing events are you overlooking?

---

16. "Black swan theory," *Wikipedia*, last modified August 12, 2012 (12:08), http://en.wikipedia.org/wiki/Black_swan_theory.

84

What does your industry or sector treat as sacred (it could be an assumption, process, or goal)? Now imagine the opposite is true.

85

Thought leaders ask "why?" a lot more than "what?" or "how?" Are you asking the right questions at the start?

86

What ways can you restate a client challenge in order to come up with new, insightful thought leadership solutions?

87

Why don't you take a client
challenge to a part of your
organization whose opinions
you have never sought before,
to gain fresh insights?

88

What are you taking
for granted? Things
change constantly. Are you
examining all areas of
change for your thought
leadership platform?

89

Have none of your ideas hit
the mark yet? Stop, redefine your
clients' problems, and think again.

90

Be wary of moving too quickly into
solution mode. Have you spent enough
time asking the right questions?

91

Does your culture engender enough curiosity? What does your organization do to foster inquiry and lifelong learning?

92

What three key trends will impact your clients over the next few years, and can your thought leadership address these?

93

Do you have current content or intellectual property that could be adapted with some extra rigor into a thought leadership point of view?

94

Do you have sector experts whose insights could be backed by robust research and then packaged and leveraged as your thought leadership?

95

Are you playing it too safe?
Is your thought leadership being
sanitized by a culture of risk
aversion within your organization?

96

Creation isn't the same as
curation. It can't be rushed and is
best done in stages. What kind of
gestation period are you allowing?

97

Before you launch your thought leadership, ask, "Is this material client-centric?" Or have you fallen into the trap of making it about you?

98

What different books, magazines, and other online content could you read that will help stimulate new ideas?

99

Dana VanDen Heuvel[17] asks, "Are you focused not only on great thought leadership but what makes for great attention leadership?"

---

17. *Marketing Savant,* http://www.marketingsavant.com.

100

Is your thought
leadership point of view
creating value, stirring
debate, or challenging
existing paradigms?

Putting Into Practice

Once you've fully explored the current conversations in your industry or space, and identified what you believe to be a fruitful area for further exploration, it's time to establish the unique point of view for which you will be known.

It is here that you can establish a true competitive edge—with the requisite discipline, time, and effort. As George Bernard Shaw is reputed to have said, "Few people think more than two or three times a year; I have made an international reputation for myself by thinking once or twice a week."

Organizations that are overly focused on short-term results and instant reactions don't think too hard or too deeply. Most never consider whether they're asking the right questions in the first place. This is the territory of risk averse, "play it safe" organizations who don't stand for anything and therefore never stand apart.

Contrast that with these exemplary organizational thought leaders:

1. BMW's Activate the Future: presenting a four-part documentary series on technology, culture, and cities and how these relate to the future of mobility.
2. IBM's Smarter Planet: articulating its point of view on the challenges facing a range of industries so that they can better meet the future head-on.
3. Freshfields Bruckhaus Deringer: showcasing insights across the telecoms, media, and technology sectors, their "Mobile Matters" campaign is hosted by way of a dedicated

microsite[18] that draws from the perspectives of over 200 global legal experts.

4. Blue Dart Express (part of the DHL Group)[19]: championing corporate social responsibility in India through their "Living Corporate Responsibility" initiative dedicated to practicing sustainability, including offering environmentally friendly logistics solutions to their customers.

5. McKinsey Quarterly: benchmarking excellence in the art and science of management.

6. Sungard Availability Services (UK)[20]: establishing the importance of business resilience for organizations around issues of cloud computing, disaster recovery, and managed hosting.

As we suggest in the "Understand the Challenge" stage of our thought leadership blueprint in the Appendix (see page 143), use these and other examples to unpack how organizations have achieved their thought leadership status—and follow their lead.

---

18. "Our Insights," *Mobile Matters*,
    http://www.mobile-matters.com/our-insights.
19. "Blue Dart and DHL are Living Corporate Responsibility in India" (press release), *Blue Dart Express Limited*, February 20, 2012,
    http://www.bluedart.com/press184.html.
20. "Creating high impact thought leadership," Sourceforconsulting.com,
    http://bit.ly/creating_thought_leadership.

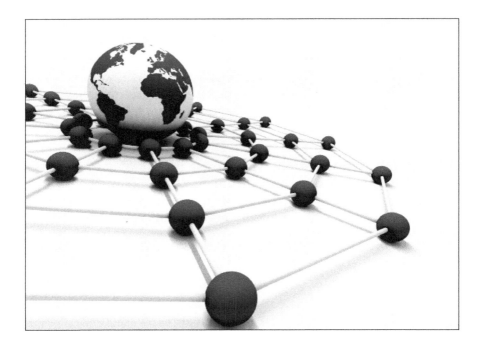

Section VI

What's Your Communication Strategy?

Building a successful thought leadership program is a long-term process. Great organizational thought leaders such as McKinsey, Accenture, IBM, and Deloitte have spent years conducting research, building market presence, and refining what works for their clients. This includes having very clear internal and external thought leadership communication strategies. Use the opportunity to address the issues raised by the following tweet-sized prompts in order to develop your own effective communication strategy.

101

The creators of your thought leadership aren't necessarily the right ones to communicate it. How will you handle this?

102

Have those who will be presenting your thought leadership across the media channels been appropriately media coached?

103

Have you coached your thought leadership champions in presentation skills so they are properly empowered to articulate your point of view?

104

Remember the #1 desire of clients: relevance. How might you customize a single piece of research to better serve specific target sectors?

105

Have you been so focused on the message that you've ignored the importance of story? Is your content engaging hearts and not just minds?

106

How frequently do you plan to communicate thought leadership messages? Will all meet the stringent criteria for what thought leadership is?

107

Have you researched what your clients read and where they source their information so you can tailor your thought leadership accordingly?

108

How do you plan to deal with outright challenges or contradictions to your thought leadership point of view?

109

Who will be involved and how in the design, development, and execution of your thought leadership campaign? Why did you choose those people?

110

Britton Manasco[21]

asks, "Are you

positioning your sales

people as thought leaders

and trusted authorities?"

---

21. Britton Manasco, "Illuminating the Future: How Thought Leaders Become Market Leaders," *Britton Manasco*, http://www.brittonmanasco.com.

111

To what extent is your sales team adequately equipped to use this thought leadership material in conversations with prospects?

112

Are people empowered to speak about your thought leadership position at every level of the company?

113

The volume of content available today is overwhelming. How have you ensured yours is smart in what, how, where, and when it is shared?

114

Consider not just what you are communicating but how you are engaging your audience visually. Have you seen the "RSA Animate" examples?[22]

22. "RSA Animate – The Power of Networks," *RSA*,
   http://comment.rsablogs.org.uk/videos/.

115

What plans have you put in place to share and celebrate the campaign's successes with everyone?

116

How are you recalibrating your messages and stories based on feedback from clients or the relevant new business team?

117

Has your thought leadership research been framed in such a way that you are able to present it as industry or sector stand-alone sections?

118

Are you examining every piece of thought leadership material in terms of how best to leverage it across all your communication platforms?

119

Have you given enough thought to how you package your thought leadership in digestible and customized ways for your clients?

120

Dale Bryce[23] asks,

"Are you ensuring your

thought leadership

facilitates a dialog? Think

of it as a conversation."

23. "Issue Two – 2012," *Sinclair Knight Merz*,
http://bit.ly/Achieve_magazine.

Putting Into Practice

Your thought leadership campaign needs focus and depth. To meet this objective, you need to pick one or two key client issues that will become your thought leadership "badge." Focus exclusively on these (as opposed to trying to cover too much ground), do a "deep dive" in ways that your competitors likely won't, and make sure you leverage and package these issues effectively.

Examine what resources you have or are prepared to invest in prior to launching your thought leadership campaign. These include funding full-time staff positions, recruiting for the necessary thinking and execution skills, as well as developing your existing employees in terms of their ability and willingness to be thought leadership champions both within and outside the organization. Think about where you might invest in partnerships with third parties with complementary capabilities, including think tanks, universities, industry associations, and research organizations, to leverage co-branding opportunities.

Consider who can help you internally and externally to execute on this campaign in order to get the message out to the right people in the right way. Your champions should be immersed in the thought leadership journey and be coached on how to deliver a compelling and consistent story.

There are two constituencies you need to leverage: internal and external.

Internal:

Your human resources team should be working with you on how best to engage your employees around your thought leadership point of view. For example, Ernst & Young in Sydney, Australia embarks on an internal launch to their employees up to six weeks before any of their thought leadership campaigns go to market.

External:

Once you have developed your content material, your focus should be on leveraging that content to the best of your ability across multiple channels and client touch points. You should be aiming for a pervasive presence across all communication channels relevant to your clients and prospects.

For example, whenever you produce a piece of well-researched thought leadership, examine whether you might package that as a short video, a blog post, an article, customer briefing, series of tweets, or discussions around the topic on relevant LinkedIn Groups and other social media sites. As Dr. Fiona Czerniawska of Source for Consulting says, "What every senior manager would like...is thought leadership that's written exclusively for them."[24] Therefore, customize your thought leadership wherever possible.

Remember, too, that your content should be varied sufficiently to match clients' and prospects' interests at different stages in the relationship cycle. That is, modify your thought leadership stance according to whether the audience has a specific need, wants to learn something new, is evaluating options, or is ready to implement a product or service.

---

24. Fiona Czerniawska, "Thought leadership in the age of mass-customisation," *The Source Blog*, May 14, 2012, **http://bit.ly/Thought_Leadership_blog**.

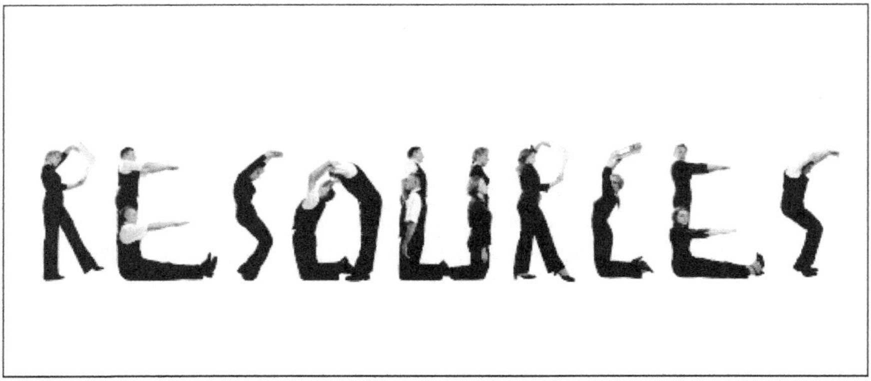
RESOURCES

Section VII

What Are the Next Steps?

We conclude this part of the book with a series of prompts that offer you specific resources and quotes from external thought leadership authorities. These are people who we recommend to help you develop and adapt your thought leadership to the ever-changing needs of your marketplace. Additionally, you'll find some final reminders to ensure that your thought leadership point of view maintains its initial high standard over time.

121

Dave Gardner asks, "Today's 'wow' is tomorrow's 'huh?' What are you doing to maintain your relevancy?"[25]

---

25. Dave Gardner, "Are you as intentional as an artist?" *Business Execution Insights* (blog), July 16, 2012, http://businessexecution.wordpress.com/2012/07/16/.

122

What books on thought leadership have you read recently? Be sure to include Craig's *Brand Stand: Seven Steps to Thought Leadership.*[26]

---

26. Craig Badings, *Brand Stand: Seven Steps to Thought Leadership* (Cooper Plains, Qld.: Book Pal, 2009).

123

Be wary of product or brand creep. Over time, are your insights sounding more like infomercials for your products or services?

124

How might writing a book help you discover *and* showcase thought leadership? Ask Liz Alexander[27] about how she helps leaders create big impact books.

27. *Dr. Liz Alexander,* http://drlizalexander.com.

125

If you are embarking on an ongoing thought leadership campaign, how are you planning to benchmark your progress year to year?

126

Have you stress tested the Key Performance Indicators you put in place and whether they are realistic? Is it time to adjust them?

127

Why are non-experts better at disruptive innovation? Naveen Jain has the answer in his *Forbes* article.[28]

---

28. Naveen Jain, "Rethinking the Concept of 'Outliers': Why Non-Experts are Better at Disruptive Innovation," *Singularity University* (Forbes.com blog), July 12, 2012 (5:05 a.m.), http://bit.ly/Forbes_Article_Rethinking.

128

Are you aware of the content at Sourceforconsulting.com,[29] focused on promoting high quality thought leadership for consultancies?

---

29. "White Space," *Source Information Services Ltd,* http://bit.ly/AboutWhiteSpace.

129

Interested in thought leadership in the B2B marketing and sales strategies space? Check out Jeff Ernst's research at Forrester.com.[30]

---

30. "Thought Leadership Marketing That Attracts Prospects To Your Thinking...And Your Funnel" (DemandGen report), *Blip*, http://bit.ly/thought_leadership_marketing.

130

Wondering how thought leaders become market leaders? Read Britton Manasco's e-zine *Illuminating the Future.*[31]

---

31. Britton Manasco, "Illuminating the Future: How Thought Leaders Become Market Leaders," *Britton Manasco*, http://www.brittonmanasco.com.

131

Mignon van Halderen[32] asks,
"Does the novelty of your
idea act as a schema-cracking
catalyst, garnering attention
& attracting stakeholders?"

32. "Dr. Mignon van Halderen," *Rotterdam School of Management, Erasmus University*, http://www.rsm.nl/people/mignon-van-halderen/.

132

Are you an entrepreneur who wants to become a thought leader? Speak to Matt Church about his *Million Dollar Expert Program.*[33]

---

33. "Matt Church – Million Dollar Expert Program," *Matt Church,* http://bit.ly/million-dollar-expert-program.

133

Looking for more industry examples of thought leadership in action? Visit the case study section of Craig's blog.[34]

---

34. "Thought Leadership – Thought Leadership case studies," "*Thought Leadership* (blog), http://bit.ly/thought_leadership_case_studies.

134

Are you aware of or, better still, have read David Meerman Scott's book *Newsjacking*?[35]

---

35. David Meerman Scott, *Newsjacking: How to Inject Your Ideas into a Breaking News Story and Generate Tons of Media Coverage* (Hoboken: John Wiley & Sons, 2011).

135

Interested in some fresh thinking on thought leadership? Read Marte Semb Aasmundsen's thesis on the topic.[36]

36. Marte Semb Aasmundsen, "Thought Leadership Thesis 2012," *Leading Thoughts* (blog), August 16, 2012 (1:26 p.m.), http://bit.ly/Thought_Leadership_Thesis.

136

The biggest challenge for over 70 percent of marketers is creating original content.[37] Why not talk to Liz Alexander about her process for doing that?

37. "Content Curation Can Inform, Engage Customers," *eMarketer*, June 4, 2012, http://bit.ly/Content_Curation_Article.

137

How has your thought leadership campaign gone so far? What has it done for your brand? What measures support the anecdotal evidence?

138

To stretch is to reach for more than what you have already accomplished. When might be a good time to adjust the goals for your campaign?

139

At the end of the day,
thought leadership—like any
performance improvement—is a
journey, not a destination. Agreed?

140

Thought leaders are brave;
explore areas others don't,
raise questions others won't, and
provide insights others can't.

Putting Into Practice

In their classic work *Surpassing Ourselves: An Inquiry into the Nature and Implications of Expertise*, cognitive scientists Carl Bereiter and Marlene Scardamalia retell the joke about the pilot who announces, "I have some bad news and some good news. The bad news is that we're lost. The good news is that we're ahead of schedule."[38] They point out that while this might not be a reassuring situation for passengers, it is an entirely appropriate conception of progress for any creative endeavor.

Think of your thought leadership as a journey, not a destination. Certainly, it's important to define your overall direction and the business outcomes you want your thought leadership to help you achieve. Just be careful not to fall into the habit of predetermining what you intend to offer. Trust the process highlighted in this book to allow for the *discovery* of those creative solutions; let them emerge.

It is one thing to articulate goals of which you are already aware and quite another to reformulate problems at new, higher levels of thinking. While there are many benefits to hiring, developing, and rewarding experts within your organization, the knowledge and beliefs we establish in these roles often blind us to what is still to be discovered.

What can help ensure you move beyond the myopic viewpoints of in-house expertise is to engage outsiders who will benefit your thought leadership *because* they aren't so completely steeped in your business, or who can help you come at the process from a different angle.

---

38. Carl Bereiter and Marlene Scardamalia, *Surpassing Ourselves: An Inquiry into the Nature and Implications of Expertise* (Chicago: Open Court, 1993).

- Knowing the right questions to ask is crucial to effective thought leadership, so who can help you find the right questions?
- Maintaining a strategic focus is crucial to effective thought leadership, so who can help you avoid getting bogged down with day-to-day tactical responses?

As Frans Johansson illustrated in *The Medici Effect: Breakthrough Insights at the Intersection of Ideas, Concepts, and Cultures*, it is the non-expert operating at the "intersection" of ideas that revolutionizes industries.[39] Don't try and go it alone. Consider an array of perspectives not just within your organization, but outside it too.

Still looking for insights on how best to take action on developing an ethos of thought leadership in your organization? In the Appendix that follows, you will find a series of proven stages to help you kick-start your journey so that you can more confidently design *and* execute your thought leadership campaign.

39. Frans Johansson, *The Medici Effect: Breakthrough Insights at the Intersection of Ideas, Concepts, and Cultures* (Boston, Mass.: Harvard Business School Press, 2004).

APPENDIX

How to Successfully Execute Your Thought Leadership Point of View

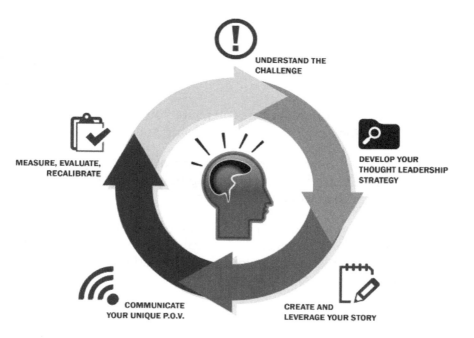

Figure A

The 140 tweet-sized prompts offered throughout this book will—as long as you act on them—help you address every aspect of an effective thought leadership campaign. This question-led methodology will assist you in arriving at the best possible thought leadership position for your organization.

Overlay it with the following five-step thought leadership blueprint (see Figure A) in order to feel wholly confident about the action you are taking to launch your thought leadership campaign.

1. **Understand the challenge**

   Use the "START IP" approach outlined below to kick-start your thought leadership planning (adapted from *Brand Stand: Seven Steps to Thought Leadership*[40]):

   a. **S**can the media and the web for content in the space that you want to own.

   b. **T**rack your competitors to ensure you are not entering an already busy thought leadership space.

   c. **A**nalyze the vision and true north of your company to ensure your thought leadership point of view is not at odds with your existing culture.

   d. **R**eview your existing intellectual property (IP). If you have existing pockets of IP, explore whether these could form the platform for your thought leadership point of view.

   e. **T**rend spot. Identify the trends most likely to impact your sector, especially your clients. Explore whether your thought leadership point of view could provide further insights or help reinterpret these trends.

---

40. Craig Badings, *Brand Stand: Seven Steps to Thought Leadership* (Cooper Plains, Qld.: Book Pal, 2009).

f.   Identify the thought leadership champions within your organization and include them in the planning as well as execution phases, coaching them appropriately to deliver your thought leadership material.

g.   Panel. Explore how you might set up an external body of experts who act as an unbiased filter and sounding board for your thought leadership approach.

Once you have completed START IP, ensure that you carefully and clearly identify whom you want to reach and the issues that most concern them.

Review both quantitative (e.g., statistics) and qualitative (e.g., case studies) research concerning your target audience, such as: What keeps them awake at night? What challenges do they struggle with the most?

Don't be afraid to "stand on the shoulders of giants" by finding the best examples of thought leadership (many of which have been outlined in this book) and copying those elements most applicable to your campaign.

Set clear business objectives. Determine what you want to achieve from your thought leadership position and clearly articulate your business objectives in a way that your champions and your entire organization understand. That way everyone will be able to adopt the broader thought leadership perspective and know how to adapt it to their everyday activities.

Establish the engagement of senior executives from the outset. Their commitment to this thought leadership campaign is vital to its success. You will ensure organization-wide buy-in if it's truly a case of "do as I do," not just "do as I say."

2. **Develop your thought leadership strategy**

Having undertaken Step 1, it's ideally time to host a workshop to develop your thought leadership strategy, at which you can draw together all the elements (including selected thought leadership champions from across the organization) necessary to your campaign. This will give you an opportunity to review whether you have the right resources to make your proposed thought leadership approach work—and to allocate them effectively.

Use the workshop format to involve *all* players. Having already aligned your overall business and thought leadership objectives, this is an opportunity to set Key Performance Indicators (KPIs) for each member of the team and specify the anticipated Return on Investment (ROI).

Following (or around the same time as) this workshop, you should—if appropriate—brief your research agency. Make sure you commission the right agency by asking to see other research they have conducted, preferably related to previous thought leadership campaigns. It is important you choose a research house that fully understands the content outputs you need to make your thought leadership campaign a success.

3. **Create and leverage your story**

Now comes the fun part: producing the content and insights that will form the backbone of your campaign. Make sure you design multiple ways to leverage and "sweat" your content. Don't be satisfied with just one report, a press release, and a client event at which you present your thought leadership function—that is merely the start.

You should be examining every possible way to leverage your content as widely as possible. Frame your research to address different sectors or split it up in such a way that you produce mini reports covering different topic areas. This will also give you fresh opportunities to send out press releases and new speaking topics for the trade publications, business organizations, and associations linked to those particular market sectors.

Once your research or point of view has been framed, make sure you turn it into a compelling story, not just a list of facts and figures. Most importantly, ensure that your thought leadership champions and your client-facing employees (such as your sales or new business teams) are well versed in that story, know how to deliver it well (perhaps through additional training), and are fully aware of what thought leadership collateral is available to them to share with clients and prospects.

4. **Communicate your unique point of view**

The excitement should be building by this point, as you are now ready to launch your thought leadership campaign. With a thought leadership communications plan in place, your objective now is to build a pervasive presence for your point of view with *all* the people you want to reach.

While the use of external channels such as social media, mainstream media, client events, launches, talks, marketing collateral, and the like are critical, don't underestimate how important it is to include your own employees as an invaluable audience for these communications. They will be your best ambassadors if they are on board and feel like part of the overall campaign and may self-identify as potential future champions.

One of the key objectives of your campaign should be to build a culture of thought leadership throughout the organization. Like any culture initiative, whether it is one related to innovation or sales, this doesn't just happen by itself. Instead, you will need to embed a focused internal engagement strategy that requires cross-disciplinary interaction (involving finance, human resources, sales, marketing, operations, corporate affairs, and so on), planning, and support throughout the business.

5. **Measure, evaluate, and recalibrate**

We're mentioning this last, but it's certainly not to be treated as "least"—or left until your thought leadership campaign is underway or in its final stages. Don't treat your thought leadership like a tick-box exercise in which you are content with vague, anecdotal assessments such as: "Successful launch (check), good media coverage (check), some high potential client meetings (check), and an engaged sales team (check)—so this thought leadership campaign must have worked and we can move on."

You need to ensure that you are assessing at every stage in your campaign whether your business objectives were met and that people have achieved their KPIs. Make sure you have feedback mechanisms in place internally and externally to measure the extent to which your thought leadership campaign has had the desired impact with respect to the bigger mission and vision of your organization. Then feed these findings back to your internal team and external partners (such as your Expert Panel—see START IP) or research agency in order to identify what worked and what didn't, so you can recalibrate your efforts going forward. These are all important activities that will not only keep your thought leadership campaign on track, but strengthen and improve it for the following period.

Thought leadership should never be thought of as a short-term, on-off campaign. Exemplars of great thought leadership— such as McKinsey, Dove's Campaign for Real Beauty, IBM's Smarter Planet, GE's Healthymagination and Ecomagination initiatives, Booz & Company's Global Innovation 1000, and Philips' Health & Wellbeing—all have campaigns that have been running for at least four years.

Finally, all that is left for us to say is good luck! Thought leadership is a courageous stance for any organization to take and best left to those who are prepared to challenge the status quo, to ask the questions no one else is prepared to ask, and to think and do things differently. Those safe havens of risk aversion and "siloed" thinking that are prevalent in far too many organizations sound the death knell for thought leadership.

It is time to break the mold and truly differentiate your brand. If you do and do it well—by embracing the insights, approaches, and resources found in this book and beyond— the rewards are likely to be huge.

What Are Your Ahas?

Thank you for reading
#THOUGHT LEADERSHIP tweet!
Got any "ahas" that would fit with this book?

We'd love to read them! Please send us your ahas
by visiting the following URL:

http://tinyurl.com/whatareyourahas

About the Authors

Dr. Liz Alexander's (*@DrLizAlexander*) gift and passion is helping to leverage an individual, team, or organization's thought leadership, using the book development process as a catalyst. Liz draws on her 25 years of experience as an international consultant, educator, marketer, business journalist, and broadcaster to help corporate executives and other experts produce critically and commercially successful thought leadership books. She had a distinguished career in the UK as a speaker and workshop facilitator, working with clients ranging from Cathay Pacific Airways to the British government's Appeals Service, before moving to the U.S. in 2001. Liz works part of the year with aspiring business authors in India.

Liz is the author of 14 nonfiction books with a global reach of close to a million readers in 20 countries. In addition to consulting and speaking throughout the United States and India, Liz developed and teaches the Strategic Communication Certificate Program for The University of Texas at Austin's Professional Development Center. She earned her PhD in Educational Psychology from UT Austin. Her website is http://drlizalexander.com and she can be reached at info@drlizalexander.com.

Craig Badings is passionate about thought leadership, having witnessed first hand the power this strategy can deliver to brands and individuals. He has spent 25 years consulting with global and local brands about their communication and thought leadership strategies. Today, he speaks and consults on how companies and individuals can employ thought leadership to truly differentiate their brand in the eyes of their target audience.

Over the past six years, Craig has conducted intense research on thought leadership and has written extensively on the topic. His book, *Brand Stand: Seven Steps to Thought Leadership*, is the first thought leadership book to outline a methodology on how to arrive at a thought leadership position.

Craig is a director of Sydney-based Cannings Corporate Communications, a member company of the ASX-listed STW Group, Australia's largest communications services group. Visit his thought leadership blog at **www.thoughtleadershipstrategy.net** and e-mail him at **cbadings@cannings.net.au**.

Liz and Craig are available individually or jointly to design and facilitate thought leadership development events for you or your organization anywhere in the world. Contact them today to discuss your needs.

Liz Alexander, PhD
http://drlizalexander.com
info@drlizalexander.com

Craig Badings
http://www.thoughtleadershipstrategy.net
cbadings@cannings.net.au

Books in the THiNKaha® Series

The THiNKaha book series is for thinking adults who lack the time or desire to read long books, but want to improve themselves with knowledge of the most up-to-date subjects. THiNKaha is a leader in timely, cutting-edge books and mobile applications from relevant experts that provide valuable information in a fun, Twitter-brief format for a fast-paced world.

They are available online at **http://thinkaha.com** or at other online and physical bookstores.

THiNKaha® Learning/Training Programs Designed to Take You to the Next Level NOW!

THiNKaha® delivers high-quality, cost-effective continuous learning in easy-to-understand, worthwhile, and digestible chunks. Fifteen minutes with a THiNKaha® book will allow readers to have one or more "aha" moments. Spending less than two hours a month with a THiNKaha® Learning Program (either online or in person) will provide learners with an opportunity to truly digest the topic at hand and connect with gurus whose subject-matter expertise gives them an actionable roadmap to enhance their skills.

Offered online, on demand, and/or in person, these engaging programs feature gurus (ours and yours) on such relevant topics as Leadership, Management, Sales, Marketing, Work-Life Balance, Project Management, Social Media and Networking, Presentation Skills, and other topics of your choosing. The "learning" audience, whether it is clients, employees, or partners, can now experience high-quality learning that will enhance your brand value and empower your company as a thought leader. This program fits a real need where time and the high cost of developing custom content are no longer an option for every organization.

> *"This program has been very successful and in demand within Cisco. The vision and implementation of the THiNKaha Learning Program has enabled us to offer high-quality content both live and on-demand. Their gurus and experts are knowledgeable and very engaging."*
>
> *- Bette Daoust, PhD*
> *Former Learning and Development Manager, Cisco, and Internal Program Manager for THiNKaha Guru Series*

Visit THiNKaha® Learning Program at http://thinkaha.com/learning.

Just **THiNK**...

- **C**ontinuous Employee/Client/Prospect Learning
- **O**ngoing Thought Leadership Development
- **N**otable Experts Presenting on Relevant Topics
- **T**ime Your Attendees Can Afford – 15 min. to 2 hrs/mo.
- **I**nformation Delivered in Digestible Chunks
- **N**ame the Topic—We Help You Provide Expert Best Practices
- **U**nderstand and Implement the Takeaways
- **I**nternal Expertise Shared Externally
- **T**raining/Prospecting Cost Decreases, Effectiveness Increases
- **Y**ou Win, They Win!

CPSIA information can be obtained at www.ICGtesting.com
Printed in the USA
LVOW011651080313

323412LV00024B/717/P